Our Own Freedom

Photographs by Maggie Murray
Introduction and comments by
Buchi Emecheta

Sheba Feminist Publishers

Our Own Freedom first published in Great Britain in
1981 by Sheba Feminist Publishers, 488 Kingsland Road,
London E8.

ISBN 0 907 179 09 6
Designed by An Dekker
Typeset in Garamond by Frances and Julia at Range Left
Photosetters, 01–251 3959.
Printed in Great Britain by
Redwood Burn Ltd., Trowbridge, Wiltshire, and
bound by Pegasus Bookbinding, Melksham, Wiltshire.

For the women of Africa and especially the Women's Group of OFREY Village, Yatenga Province, Upper Volta.

Acknowledgements

Firstly, I want to thank all those people who helped me to understand the meaning of many things I have seen and photographed, especially . . .

Madame Azetout

Adama & Bernard Ouedraogo

Ayo McIver

Violet Gumbleton

Val Wilmer

and Buchi Emecheta, whose contribution to the book has been immeasurable.

The ideas and facts in this book come from many sources and innumerable hours spent talking. Barbara Rogers' book, *The Domestication of Women – Discrimination in Developing Societies*, (Pub. Kogan Page) is central to the argument. I have used extracts from her articles and from others in the United Nations Report, *The State of the World's Women 1979*. Peter Sullivan's charts are reproduced courtesy of the Report.

Despite reservations, I found *North–South. A Programme for Survival* (The Brandt Report) a useful source of reference and have quoted from it.

The extracts from Mariam Matiko's article used courtesy of *New African*, magazine.

I would like to acknowledge the help and support of Christian Aid and Ikon Productions for whom I took many of the photographs. Over the years, too, *New Internationalist* magazine has provided me with much information about development.

Finally, I would like to thank all those women who looked after, and entertained my child while I worked on this book.

Maggie Murray, July 1981.

Contents

'Women and girls constitute one-half of the world population and one-third of the official labour force, perform nearly two-thirds of work hours, but according to some estimates, receive only one-tenth of the world's income and less than one-hundredth of world property'.

● *Women at Work*, International Labour Organization report.

A Kikuyu woman in the Highlands of Kenya. Her husband has gone South to work in a factory. Because she is supporting a bundle of firewood — using a traditional Kikuyu headstrap — she carries her baby in front. Collecting wood for fuel is mainly a woman's task. It can take hours every day. This woman also runs the family farm, does all the household chores and brings up six children.

Introduction

In Nigeria, where I grew up, only one's enemies would make a special prayer for the birth of a girl child. The normal prayers would go, 'You will be safely delivered of a bouncing baby boy, a real man-child, on a large banana leaf, so that we can come and make jolly with plenty of palm wine and pounded yam'. The pregnant woman would not protest to this prayer because in her heart she too would like to have a man child who would not be married away but would stay in the family's homestead and look after his mother when she became old and weak. In most African societies, the birth of a son enhances a woman's authority in the family: male children are very, very important.

One of the human survival qualities is adaptation. If after all the prayers, the woman in question has a girl child, she is at first disappointed, and then welcoming and warm towards her new baby. Her husband probably receives the news with indifference, then resignation. In London, one African student husband shouted in desperation, 'Shio, wasted nine months'!

But would there be any survival at all, if there were no female babies? The new mother who wanted a son had a mother; the young husband who shouted, 'Shio, wasted nine months', was delivered by a woman. Still many people regard the birth of a female child as almost a failure.

A child is named according to the circumstances surrounding its birth. Girls are more so. They are given names that express the family's expectation that a girl will grow up to be a good helper and a bringer of wealth. Of the major African tribes, Yorubas give names like 'Rike', meaning 'I have this one to pet'. Another tribe would say, 'Ogoli bu uno', meaning 'Woman is the maker of home'. Some Ibos would go straight to the point and name their daughters 'Ego Obi' meaning, 'Obi's money'. Obi is usually the male head of the family. So this child could grow and keep herself well, knowing that on her wedding night her bride price would go to the Obi. On the other hand, a common Ibo name for a male child is 'Nkencho', meaning, 'This is the one I want', or, 'This is the sex I want'.

A girl child comes into her own very, very early in life. By the age of five, she has an 'in-built' desire to work and help her family out, as if somehow she were aware of the disappointment she has caused her parents simply by being a girl. The collection of photographs in this book shows that the basic things of life — water, fire, shelter, the care of the young and sick, the growing of food — are almost entirely done by women. These are the basic necessities of life, and yet there is little or no compensation to the women who do them. Because they are unpaid, such tiring and boring chores are called 'women's jobs'. A girl who dares to grumble is reminded, 'But you are a woman'. That usually shuts her up. A little girl has her own gourd or bucket for fetching water. This may sound strange to women in highly industrialised societies, where one has only to turn on the tap for clean water. In many countries of the world, this is still a luxury. Little girls may have to trek for miles every morning to get the family's water. Fetching firewood for daily cooking is a major job. Women and young girls go miles into the bush, cut free the dry stems of the African bush with the cutlasses they always carry, tie them together with strong twigs and carry them, mostly on their heads, back to the family compound. Sometimes respected senior wives in some tribes are not permitted to carry things on their heads. So such honoured women have to use either their backs or their shoulders. Their heads have become sacred because they are the senior wives of important men. But they still carry firewood and water.

A hardworking female child of six or eight never goes without praise. Her father would at this stage come to value her. She would fetch for him, fill his pipe, help in cooking his food. Here you see men, sitting far off watching the industrious girl or young woman. One then hears the men remark, 'She works so hard, almost like a man, or just like my mother'. When a clever wife hears this about her daughter, she knows better than to say, 'But she was a case of a wasted nine months'. In her early teens, unless she is at school, the father is forced to give up the daughter he has now learnt to love and rely on. One wonders sometimes whether there is an inherent bitterness in letting them go. There are always arguments about the amount of a bride price. In places where there are dowries, the bride's father is always envious of the new husband's relatives, since a useful daughter is going away from the family. The bride price or bride wealth, as the modern African man likes to call it, is an attempt to recover the lost services of an industrious daughter.

In her new home, a girl continues with exactly what she was doing in her father's house. She wakes up early in the morning, goes down to the stream with the other women in her new compound, fetches her water for the day, not forgetting to have her bath. Then she treks back and cooks her husband's morning meal. If she is married into a polygamous

compound, her work is multiplied, because she has to cook and fetch water for many more people. If she is lucky, some grown up daughters of her new compound help her. She is given her own farm, which she keeps in good condition with the farm tools her mother has given her. On her way back from the farm, she brings the vegetables and firewood for her new family.

In most non-Christian communities, women have a big market day every five days. On this day, the housewife takes some of her farm products to the market to sell. She uses the money to buy fish, soap and hair oil, and she takes part in local gossip and dancing. The market for most African women is much more than a place to buy and sell.

Village life is becoming modified in many places. During my recent visit to Nigeria, I found that the educated village farmer still insists on paying a heavy bride price for his wife because, as one university student said, 'You don't feel you own your wife until you have paid heavily for her head'. But many such men do give a small amount of money for buying fish, meat and children's clothes. In most cases however, the farmland is still the housekeeping money.

The young wife's work increases when children start to arrive. Her mother or an old relative who lives in the compound may take care of the young baby while the mother works the farm. In some places on the Gambia, the new father builds a shed on the farm in which the mother can rest and breastfeed her baby when it gets too hot. He also builds a small raised basket, as a cot for the napping baby. But in most cases, mothers prefer to back their babies. They prefer to know where the baby is and what it is up to. They prefer backing because then they can tell when the baby is feverish, thirsty or simply wants an extra cuddle. On the emotional level, the mother's warmth radiates to the child — the child feels secure, safe, confident of its mother's love. I like listening to mothers sing to their babies when they are busy cutting grass for new buildings in Cross River's State of Southern Nigeria. Sometimes a mother will stop her work, rock the child on her back to the rhythm of a song, and then go back to her work again. Women who work this way are paid daily.

Little children, male or female, are the prerogatives of women. In families where there are many wives, the women look after all the children in the compound in turns. Wife number one cooks for a specific time for the whole family, and during this time the husband sleeps in her hut or in the part of the compound that belongs to her. She also looks after all the children at this time. Then it is the turn of the next one in line. The husband can stay with the senior wife any time he feels like it, and in cases where there are more than three wives, she may not be expected to take part in the cooking at all.

The senior wife has a privileged position. The fact that she is free from tedious farm work and the boring carrying and fetching of water and cooking for a large family, leaves her time to concentrate on developing her personality. If she is lucky to be blessed with sons, she becomes a very strong person in her family and is respected in her community. She can speak boldly in the gathering of their community. Such women tend to be so intelligent and fearless that they are thought to be almost 'as good as men' in their public duties. Many such women become big local traders and earn quite a lot. Most of the profit, however, goes back to the family in the form of school fees for the sons. If a senior wife is really well to do, her daughters can benefit by going to Institutes of Further Education. Hence a young wife who grumbles about her husband's second wife is always reminded, 'But you are the first wife', because this means a great deal. Where there is no will after the father's death, the children of the first wife, who invariably would be older, usually inherit most of his property. The sons of the second and subsequent wives are given little shares, if the first son of the first wife is kind. He is not obliged to share, in most West African tribal societies. This pattern is different among some tribes in Ghana, where inheritance comes through the female side, but one fact remains: the inheritance usually goes through the oldest female – the daughter of the first wife – unless she is childless.

In agrarian societies, polygamous life works because it results in more hands to work on the farm. Also no child is without a family. Men chase and look for women, not the other way round, so every woman must marry: one of the reasons why such places have child brides. Prostitution among women is rare, and bachelor girls are seldom heard of. But one single man can have as many as a hundred or so children and still to be free to inherit his dead brother's wife. Such arrangements are fast becoming impossible. Many people drift into towns where accommodation is difficult to find, and there are no farms in the big cities for the third or fourth wife to work on. Polygamous life is gradually dying out among the farmers, but the new wealthy Moslem class in rich countries like Nigeria, and some areas on the Gambia, is giving it a new life. University-educated women willingly marry a wealthy man, even though he has two other wives. Marriage gives them the protection of his wealth, his name and position. Some men even make wills now to protect the children of the younger wives. The argument is that if university girls do not marry such men, the chances are that they will never marry. In societies where marriage and children are the most honourable career women can hope for, one understands why women would rather have these arrangements than live alone.

The older a woman gets, the more respect she commands. As there is no social security of any kind for all the work she has spent a whole life doing, her children, especially the sons, now take it upon themselves to

look after their mother. Her words are listened to with reverence, and her daughters-in-law leave their children with her. Most of these old ladies become reflective, so much so that they become living history books. They tell stories and sing songs of their historic past. They string together praise-names and retell the happenings of their community over and over again. (I was determined to be a story teller as a little girl, after listening for many years to the stories told by my father's mother in our village in Ibusa, in Southern Nigeria.) Nobody paid these women for their services until it was realised that one could write such things in books. Men have now taken over this role and are now being paid for it. A few women, like the present writer, are now beginning to find their way back into the art of story telling, which was once a 'woman's job'.

Most of these village functions are now being eroded. Old ladies in the urban city centres are now becoming headaches for their offspring due to the scarcity of adequate accommodation. From the photos on pages 66–70, it becomes clear that women can no longer strap their babies behind their backs in factories and in their low paid jobs in the urban city centres. This is a pity. The emotional warmth and closeness the village child derives from its mother is going up in factory smoke. It is debatable if these women, the urban poor, are better off in the cities than in the villages. Many women are left to care for their children alone. Not that this is very strange to the African women, who have shouldered the care of their young for a very long time. But the new care of children in the cities is different from that of the village. The children have no compounds to belong to. They are cramped in a one room apartment, with the mother alone acting as the father, the mother, the compound head, the grandmother and all those community relatives of the extended family, which a village child has as its birthright. Women in places like Lesotho, and in many places in Southern Africa, had been living like this for decades. The men are out working in the mines, and when they do come to the village for a visit, they usually leave the woman with another pregnancy and take the little food there is with them back to town. The men are not to blame in cases of this kind, because the apartheid laws were formulated by their white masters. These laws breed new sets of women: the mother with her dependent children in the village trust land, and the young woman in the shanty parts of the city with unwanted children to look after.

In the big cities, the problem of childcare is also becoming acute. For economic reasons, more and more families are becoming monogamous. The old village lady can no longer come and live with her children in the city, because of lack of accommodation. As most workplaces do not like children on the premises, greater economic strain is being put upon the not-so-educated female. On the farm, she had her self-respect, in that she contributed to the family's income. Now she is entirely dependent on her man. In some big cities, this has intensified wife battering. Unlike the extended family interference of the villages, city neighbours do not interfere. Some women are now forming nursery cooperatives in which they take it in turns to look after their babies, or in which they pay one of their members to look after the babies while the others go out to work in the factories.

The success of this kind of arrangement becomes a matter of class. We are beginning to have trained professional women, though in comparison with the rest of the population, their number is still very small. Until quite recently, school fees were very heavy, and parents would rather invest in their sons than in daughters who would eventually marry and leave the family to go and enrich somebody else. But many West African countries are now introducing free primary education. It is not compulsory in many African countries, and the parents are free to make a choice. Would the girl be more useful helping her mother at home or in her market trade, or would she benefit from education? And if the family decided that she would be better off at school, could the family afford to pay the fees? And how long should she stay at school? In the semi-industrial cities, a girl's future depends on the decision of her parents. Girls are even more valuable among the Moslem communities. In most cases her mother would be an *eleha*, the West African version of being in purdah. Some of these women still wear shaddock. They live in large communal compounds and are seldom seen outside. Their young daughters are usually 'their feet' and 'their eyes'. Mothers, even though they live such sheltered lives, still trade, through their young daughters who hawk their mother's products on the streets. The profit goes back to the family budget.

The family budget is always a bone of contention. Men claim that women make all this money and spend it on themselves. 'Themselves', in the real sense of the word, usually means one's children. Women who for lack of suitable education can't go out to work do some petty trading. They usually have small children with them. They trade in anything. It could vary from a few loaves of bread to just a packet of matches or two. Some lucky ones have stalls or sheds, others not so fortunate use the front of their houses for their stalls. Many Nigerian women living in the big cities collect their little profits as *esusu* or partner (West Indian women in Britain perfected this method of compulsory saving: they call it *padner*). Each woman pays a certain sum of money every week or month, and the whole collection is given to a member. The collection rotates. Many women use this to build up a little capital with which to boost their trade. So a woman could start by taking and selling sixty loaves of bread a week, and move on to selling three hundred, because now she has more

capital to put into her trade, and in many cases she can now afford to hire a girl hawker or rent a stall. Some men see this gradual growth of domestic economy as a challenge. They say women are richer than they, who have to go to the offices or factories every day, taking insults from annoying bosses.

In some cases women who start in this humble way do get rich. But the word 'rich' is very relative. All told her capital may not be much, but she looks rich because she can afford to clothe herself the way she wants. She can afford to buy things for her children, and maybe send a few pounds to her parents. To achieve all this, she would have to be very frugal. But what shows through to any observer is her independence and satisfaction. When her husband can't stop her, he simply accepts the situation. Many women have survived the strains of the city this way. When observers come to big Nigerian towns like Ibadan, they see everybody trading. People used to wonder and say, 'But who buys from whom, when everybody trades?' But people buy from each other because neighbours don't normally trade in the same commodities.

Some women go further than this, by forming themselves into traders' co-operatives. They can become so powerful that they monopolise the import of certain commodities in certain areas. These women are now cynically called the 'Tick Madams' (Thick madams) in Lagos. They build houses and have great influence in local politics. Due to lack of formal education, they don't become top politicians, but their influence is important in getting votes for the local senator. The older ones, like the older women in the villages, can be very outspoken. No longer busy being 'women', they can now afford to be themselves. Money and hard work have placed them in positions of respect.

There are some women lucky enough to come from families who value formal education for women. Many schools, convents and training colleges now exist for women and young girls. About a third of West African girls now have some basic schooling. Some go to Arabic schools. Many of these girls go on to further training to become real professionals in the Western sense of the word. Like the early educated women in Europe, women still tend to go out and do the jobs they do at home. Nursing, teaching and cooking are favourite professions. Those who go into offices go as secretaries, again helping men to get on. Apart from the fact that most of these professions are home extensions, they do not demand long periods of training. As has been said earlier, most girls' ultimate ambition is to marry. Going into a long period of apprenticeship would be a hindrance. After school hours, girls come home to help with the housework. So the concentration which a boy could afford to give his school work is denied the girls. A few women are managing to break these barriers by sheer determination to get on, or like the present writer, by educating themselves after their babies are born.

The real professional woman is still something new. She is a salaried person who knows that she is not inferior in intelligence. She, like her sisters all over the world, has to carry the double yoke of being intelligent, a role that some men say is not attractive in women, and still having to be a wife and mother. In West Africa she still wants to marry and have children. Few of her generation would say, like some of their sisters in the Western world, 'I find fulfilment in my work and don't think I want children'.

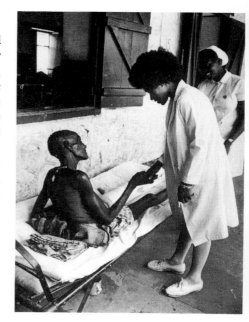

Men still shy away from professional women. Remember the university student who wants to pay the bride price so that he can own and command respect? How much can a man pay for the head of a qualified doctor to earn *her* respect, say? Professional women tend to marry fellow students or very rich businessmen. And the rate of divorce is high. The women's contribution to the economy of the society is just too obvious – everybody knows the scales of salaries paid to top executives. It has been said that the values of any society are the values of the ruling class. The ruling class in West African societies consists of men. And these men regard women as inferior. Because of this, the work women do, though valued and regarded as very necessary, is, like the women who do it, not expected to be taken on the same level as the work done by men. 'Women's jobs' are looked down on. Because of this, work done by women is not very well paid, because according to the values of the society, they are low jobs. So runs the circular argument.

In many ways, nature seems to be on the side of the ruling class, the men. African women crave and want children. Some say that this is a natural yearning, but this is doubtful. What happens is that a girl child is conditioned right from birth into seeing her main role as that of wife and mother. She is brought up to think that without children, she is not a full woman. During each pregnancy, she feels euphoria at achieving the greatest job she is put on this earth for. So any minor role given to her by the society at this time, she accepts simply to fill her time. The human infant we know is dependent on its mother for a longer time than most other mammals. So the mother tugs her infant along, and this is very hampering. As soon as she weans child number one she would want another one, because in her society, her future is not secure otherwise.

Bearing and rearing children takes much of a lifetime, and the women are not paid. So apart from farm work, village women contribute directly to the economy. Yes, it takes a man and a woman to make a child, but only the woman carries the unborn child, and only she nurses it and raises it. With this 'full time job', she cannot engage in 'men's work', which is much more highly valued. Even the professional woman is finding that child rearing puts her at a disadvantage in comparison to her male colleagues. By the time she has passed childbearing age, her male colleagues are all set in their professions, while she may need to re-join and start all over again. But for her part, she has secured the next generation, for which she is not paid. Hopefully she will live to see old age and maybe be remembered by the children for whom she gave the best part of her life.

In Western countries, family and child benefits, free schooling (with free uniforms for those who need them) help women who have to look after their children alone. More men now want to take a share in the rearing of their children. In Britain, family benefits carry the mother's name. This is not so in Africa.

The woman's job is not appreciated, and when there is any foreign aid, it usually goes to the heads of family, again men. Apart from imported food stuffs like tinned milk, which is specially for children, all other types of aid go to the men. Some heads of families sell their share of aid products to make 'more money' rather than using them for their immediate family, for whom they were intended.

The other side of the argument is that most African men are not free. That when they are economically free, they will value the work done by women. That when there is enough money, girls, like boys, will be educated, and with education people's attitude will change. Like women in Southern Africa, most African women are expected to wait until our menfolk are free before we start talking of our own freedom. But maybe by the time they get their own freedom, and then decide that it is time for us to get ours, we'll be dead. Why make women wait for these attitudes to change? Some countries in West Africa are not that poor, and yet the society is very patriarchal.

Many factors are responsible. Those West African countries colonised by the British were colonised during the Victorian era, an era in which a woman, like her child, was expected to be seen and not heard. The British have gone, but their influence is still very present. So the modern changes of women's position in the western world will take a very long time to percolate into the consciousness of the Africans. As has been said earlier, in her traditional society, woman had a role, a difficult one, but still a role that made her feel like a person in her community. Now with the big towns taking the place of such communities, such roles are being denied her. So she is now trapped between the traditional and the modern.

One major thing still exists – she still has to bear and rear her children. And whether she has to go to her farm to get food to feed her children, or into a city factory, or become a prostitute to get money for her children, the African woman feels it is her duty to produce and breed the next generation. It is a role she hands on to her daughter. With the help of family planning clinics, child clinics and dispensaries, her work is becoming easier. It is great work that people take for granted. For the women of Africa it is still not easy.

These women, unsung, need more help and appreciation than they now get.

These photographs show many of the methods these women use to keep their society alive. They show that living in Africa as a woman is still a hard, hard work.

Buchi Emecheta, 1981

The seventeen hour day

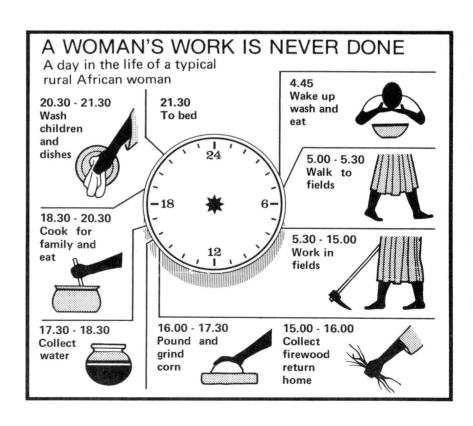

A WOMAN'S WORK IS NEVER DONE
A day in the life of a typical rural African woman

20.30 - 21.30
Wash children and dishes

21.30
To bed

4.45
Wake up wash and eat

5.00 - 5.30
Walk to fields

18.30 - 20.30
Cook for family and eat

5.30 - 15.00
Work in fields

17.30 - 18.30
Collect water

16.00 - 17.30
Pound and grind corn

15.00 - 16.00
Collect firewood return home

'The UN Economic Commission for Africa estimates that between sixty per cent and eighty per cent of the labour done in the fields is done by women. Set beside the fact that eighty per cent of the African population lives directly off the land, this is a forceful reminder of the economic importance of women throughout the continent.'
● Barbara Rogers, *State of the World's Women* Report 1979 UN.

'Where there is poverty . . . it is women who suffer its worst effects. Where there is prejudice, it is women who bear the heaviest burden of discrimination. To be born female is to be born with less scope for personal development than males, with less likelihood of ever enjoying such freedoms, responsibilities and privileges as are available . . . For this reason, the women's movement will remain one of the most creative and dynamic of our times – a force for change through which the emancipation of both men and women may one day be realized . . . The problems of women are the problems of society as a whole. The whole society is affected by high rates of maternal and child mortality, and by malnutrition and illiteracy in young girls and mothers. The whole society is deprived of the creativity and wisdom of women when their talents and abilities are left undeployed.'

● Helvi Sipila. Assistant Secretary General for Social Development and Humanitarian Affairs of the United Nations, 1979.

In Southern Sudan a woman carries a local fuel, charcoal, past petrol tankers queueing to cross the Nile at Juba. Every oil price rise makes most recent Western strategies for development even more unworkable. The African farming tradition is to produce food without resorting to 'imported energy' on a large scale. We may all live to give thanks that this tradition has survived and be glad to learn from it.

'Many development objectives have added benefits if they take into account the effects on women. Two of women's arduous tasks in most poor rural areas are gathering firewood, for which they must walk further and further afield as forests are cut down, and carrying water over long distances. The providing of alternative fuels would not only help to check deforestation; it would also give women more time for education, income-generating activities and social and political participation. Clean and more convenient water supplies would provide similar benefits for women, as well as being vital for health.'

● Brandt Report. *North-South: A Programme for Survival* 1980.

The Brandt Commission Report, 'North South' was published in 1980 and got worldwide attention. The commission was set up at the suggestion of Robert McNamara, President of the World Bank and Willie Brandt, the West German politician. Its view is liberal and its analysis and recommendations have been rightly treated with caution and criticism by many countries outside the western economic block. Nevertheless it gathered together some useful information and did highlight one important fact: that although women do most of the work, particularly in rural communities, their contribution is hidden. So, many efforts for 'development' through projects and aid founder because they are directed at men who neither necessarily understand nor do the work.

'With the development of rural areas in less developed countries, subsistence agriculture based on food crops is changing to cash crops produced for the market and often on large plantations. Ploughs or tractors and better tools are introduced and usually only men have access to the training required, as well as the loans, new seeds and fertilisers.

Women lose the status, independence and income that they had with their own farms and instead do the heavier work like weeding, transplanting, hoeing and digging of these cash crops on larger farms run by men. This is in addition to work on their own family farms and all their domestic chores. Economic development in less developed countries has not yet changed the lives of most women except to increase their unskilled work.'
● *Man's World, Women's Work*. Christian Aid leaflet.

'*Even in the wage labour the men stand up while the women bend over.*'
● *Buchi Emecheta*

Farming and fieldwork

WOMEN'S WORK IS NOT RECOGNISED

National statistics for the economically active usually omit women's work in the subsistence sector yet:

 In the Himalayan region 70% of agricultural work is done by women

 In Africa 60 - 80% of all agricultural work is done by women

 Rural women in the developing countries as a whole account for at least 50% of food production

'African farming has been much maligned and its technology much underestimated by outsiders partly because African farmers proved so resistant to colonialism, development and fertilisers. African farmers have a wealth of experience relating to plants. They also have a fund of knowledge concerning the social consequences of technological change. Their ideas should be heard more often'.
● Susan and Paul Richards from 'Living with the Land'.

Cutting grass for thatching in Southern Sudan.

'In most parts of sub-Saharan Africa, women are traditionally associated with food production and the family consumes grain and vegetables produced by the adult women household members, whereas the men produce the cash crops and accrue the cash earnings. In fact, very often women perform a number of cash cropping tasks, especially drudgerous weeding, yet the cash crop is regarded as solely the man's product. He therefore almost invariably decides how the cash is to be spent, and he may very well opt not to use the money to replenish the family cooking pot.

In some villages, the only way women are afforded an opportunity to get cash is to sell home-made brews to the local menfolk and thereby get some of the male monopolised cash earnings to spend on their families' welfare.'
● Mariam Matiko in *New African* 1981.

Harvesting millet, a staple crop in N.E. Ghana. Nearly all fieldwork in Ghana is done with a small hand hoe, a machete or a knife. Recently bullocks have been introduced for ploughing. It is men who are being taught these new skills.

'In traditional society women had important rights, based on the work they did on the land. The commercialisation of the African economy, however, combined with Western-style legislation to confer outright ownership on one person (usually a man, since he would have the cash to deal in land), has seriously undermined those rights. Wholesale "land reform" is a classic example of how well-intentioned development policies which ignore women's economic role can contribute to making many people destitute or dependent, for the first time, on a man who is not accustomed to sharing out his assets . . .'

● Barbara Rogers.

Maria Gumbo harvesting beans. Kwa MKono village, Tanzania. With her husband and children she works a relatively large *shamba* (farm) growing maize and vegetables for the family and cotton as a cash crop. She also keeps goats and chickens and tends fruit trees.

'The woman who works on a farm may provide everything for her family but it is not recognized because the product is eaten. Men then have time for building huts, planting, hunting and local wage labour. Their earnings are spent on themselves, on things like bikes and alcohol. The men feel they own the things they have produced. What the woman has produced has gone. Some men do now contribute house-keeping money as they can no longer hunt. But the men still own the land.'
● *Buchi Emecheta*

'While the global community cries out against the possible starvation of millions unless food production and distribution are improved, Africa's food producers — the women — continue largely to be ignored.'
● Economic Commission for Africa.

'The watering can is a new invention for Africa. A simple thing like that can make a real difference for a person.'
● *Buchi Emecheta*

Firewood and water

Collecting water and fire-wood are generally women and children's work in Africa. These two basic and essential tasks can take hours each day. As the world's timber resources dwindle, the price of firewood in towns rises and village women have to search further and further for each day's cooking and heating fuel.

In many parts of Africa wells are shared by a group of villages and so women have to walk quite long distances to them. In times of drought, or when a well becomes polluted, women are faced with catastrophic problems. All this is classified as non-productive work.

Women of Ofrey village, Upper Volta, returning from the well.

Carrying wood for making charcoal, Southern Sudan.

Many African wells are simply a hole in the ground. This is a typical well in Upper Volta. Because it has a simple surround of tree trunks it is slippery and difficult to use at times. The risk of pollution, too, is higher than for a well with a concrete inside lining and surround.

Drinking-water on tap in a Tanzanian *ujamaa* village. These self-running co-operatives were started as part of the country's socialist policy of self-reliance. Although the programme has severe problems and has been criticised both inside and outside Tanzania, it provided a model of self-sufficiency for other parts of Africa. When people formed a co-operative village they were helped by the government to obtain clean drinking water, a dispensary and a school. Yet in socialist Tanzania the women and girls fulfil their traditional roles.

Fulani women on the edge of the Sahel. This stand pump with a concrete surround and linked but separate trough for animals, is easy to use and avoids many pollution risks. Nevertheless, too big a drilling programme in any one area has its own dangers. It can lower the water table so that new wells rapidly dry up and it can shift the ecological balance of an area by encouraging the breeding of more animals. This pump was installed during a severe drought by a joint council of local Christians and Muslims, (Islam is the majority non-African religion in most African countries north of the Equator).

Young women members of a co-operative village farming project in Northern Senegal. The water used in their village is collected from a nearby river and irrigation channels. Often people prefer river water to 'clean' well water as having more flavour.

Bringing home firewood in Central Ghana. West Africa has one of the few areas of true rain forest left in the world.

Childcare and health

Ghanaian distillery co-op. Akpeteshie is a local gin made from molasses, a by-product of sugar-refining.

Multi-national companies like Nestlés and Bristol-Myers promote powdered baby milk in Africa. Through intensive advertising campaigns they persuade mothers that 'modern' feeding-bottles are better than the breast.

Infant mortality and sickness increase as a result, since babies are often fed on milk-powder solutions which are over-diluted with polluted water and used in unsterilised bottles. It has been estimated that ten million cases a year of mal-nutrition and disease can be traced to incorrect bottle feeding. Yet despite growing international opposition the ▶

'It looks as if the baby is a girl because there is no man there. The woman may be recovering from the shock. With a boy she would be surrounded by men from the moment she sits up.'
● *Buchi Emecheta*

Village maternity unit in Upper Volta. The health worker with the mother is a local woman who has received basic medical training. She works together with the traditional midwife who has great prestige and experience. So aspects of both medical systems are exploited and the value of African medicine recognized.

35

companies refuse to accept responsibility for what they consider the 'misuse' of their product. (Baby milk sales in the Third World are worth around £700 million.)

More countries, including Kenya, are enforcing the UN code which prohibits direct advertising, free gifts to medical staff and the employment of uniformed company 'milk' nurses. At a recent (Spring 1981) World Health Organization vote on adopting the code only the USA voted against. Britain abstained.

'A beautiful child belongs to the father. A sick and ugly one belongs to the mother.'
● *Buchi Emecheta*

'... in most cases mothers prefer to back their babies. They prefer to know where the baby is and what she is up to. They prefer backing because then they can tell when the baby is feverish, thirsty or simply wants an extra cuddle. On the psychological level, the mother's warmth radiates to the child, the child feels secure, safe, confident of its mother's love.'
● *Buchi Emecheta*

Maria Gumbo and her four youngest children having breakfast of *ugali* – maize meal porridge – and tea.

Preparing food in Central Ghana. The plantain in the foreground will be pounded with cassava to make *fufu*.

Fulani women at a nutrition session. One woman was selected by the community to liaise between them and the health team which visits fortnightly. The health team consists of a nurse and a locally trained assistant. The most common serious diseases amongst the Fulani are malaria, diarrhoea, conjunctivitis and bronchitis.

For most women simple remedies and a village clinic are more valuable than a gleaming modern hospital – inaccessible and terrifying. Many of the best village health services are locally based; they involve local people trained in basic medical skills and are integrated with agricultural programmes. Preventative medicine and an understanding of basic nutrition are obviously important, but everything fails if the crops do not grow.

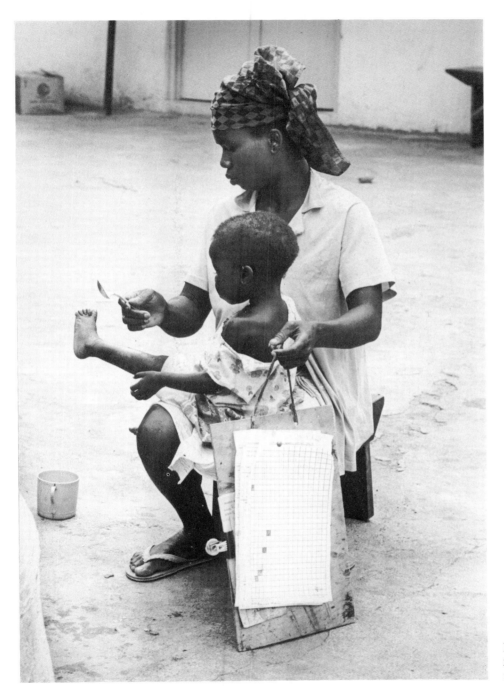

At Bawku Food and Health House in Ghana women stay for two or three weeks when they or their children are ill.

'For health drink water from a properly managed well.'

'Women bear many other hardships in the poorest countries. The greatest health hazards occur among children and pregnant women; but the design and distribution of health facilities rarely reflect this fact. This contributes to the situation observed in many low-income countries, that women's life expectancy is lower than men's (the opposite of the position in rich countries); that more than half of them suffer from anaemia; and that in some large poor countries their health appears to be worsening. But women cannot do much to improve their lot while authority and information remain in the hands of men.'
● Brandt Report.

Household tasks

Early morning, Tetrem village, Central Ghana. The home of the Fordjours, a large extended family. A man and his two wives, their twelve children ranging from two — thirty four years old, and an uncle live here. Children learn early to help women with household tasks and play an important part in servicing the family and working in the fields.

Grace Buada lives in a co-op housing scheme in Tema, Ghana. She moved from country to city with her husband, searching for work. Although their housing is very simple, it is a great improvement on their previous rented room. She is cooking on a charcoal stove made from discarded car panels. Her husband is playing draughts with a neighbour.

'Mothers handing down the future to their daughters.'
● *Buchi Emecheta*

Mrs. Cato is a headmistress in Ghana. Her husband is an executive in the United Africa Company. Although she has a 'houseboy' Mrs. Cato does the market shopping herself and cooks most of the food. Her daughter helps get the food ready, her son cooks breakfast and her husband does the supermarket shopping. She also grows some fruit and vegetables and keeps chickens.

Women all over Africa spend many hours each day milling grain into the flour which forms the basis of most diets. Traditional methods include pounding and stone grinding.

In this village, Goubré, Upper Volta, a mechanical mill has been installed which does the work in a few minutes. This was set up as a project by one of the village 'Classe d'age' (age-groups). This is a group of people who were born at around the same time, and traditionally each group takes responsibility for teaching and initiating its members. They often organize group ceremonies for important occasions – marriage and circumcision for example. The village mill was originally funded by a government development programme. The villagers will pay off this loan and also contribute towards setting up a 'child of the mill' in a nearby village.

Ofrey village, Upper Volta. Lizette Zacremba making *soumbala*, dumplings of millet and neere seeds. She dries them on the roof of the house and then uses them in soups and stews.

Market trade

Women traders start by building up capital in small ways. In the country they do this by selling surplus produce, in the town they get goods 'on tick' in order to sell them. In West Africa, particularly, some women traders become relatively rich and influential in their community. Some may be supporting children at school or university.

'The market for most African women is more than a place to buy and sell, it is a social place as well.'
● *Buchi Emecheta*

'*An established trader. Look at her face. Men fear the "tick mama". She can say what she feels. Her yams will always be sold in the same place.*'
● *Buchi Emecheta*

'Simple basic trader building up capital. The butcher would give her 12 trotters at a time "on tick". When she has built up enough capital she can buy a whole pig.'
● *Buchi Emecheta*

Araba Asemaba, Chairwoman of the Secondi-Takoradi Co-op, selling goods in the Co-op's shop. The co-operative movement has been very strong in Ghana. Some produce basic foodstuffs like rice, eggs or vegetables. Others offer services like tailoring or retailing. At this shop members can buy local produce as well as household items, drink, cigarettes and, when available, imported goods.

Maize traders in the rainy
season.

Wage labour

Women labourers on a drainage construction outside Ougadougou at dawn.

Few African women who leave traditional society manage to find skilled or semi-skilled work. As in Europe, men work in the well-paid factory jobs and learn to operate machinery. In some countries, especially socialist ones, this is beginning to change.

Women construct ninety per cent of the roads in Lesotho.

A growing number of women tractor drivers and mechanics are employed on equal terms with men on the state farms in Mozambique.

Loading sacks of rice at Tamale rice mill, Ghana. Women do outside labouring but few are employed inside the mill doing semi-skilled jobs.

Tea picking on an estate in Uganda. This is skilled work done by women and men.

'Even though she's cooking – a household chore – she cannot have her baby on her back.'
● *Buchi Emecheta*

Cooking for seven hundred and forty employees in the works canteen, Kumasi Brewery, Ghana.

Professional careers

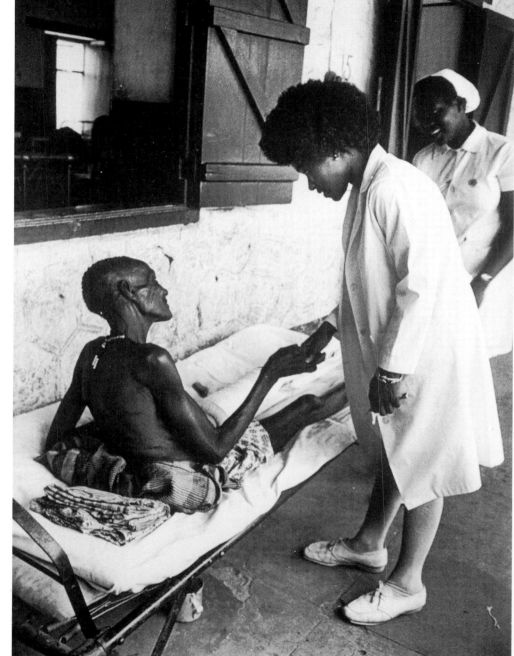

Although certain individual women have succeeded as politicians, writers, doctors etc., career employment for women in Africa follows a very similar pattern to that in Europe and the United States. There are basically three opportunities for further education leading to a career. They fit women into the caring, supportive roles which they fulfil in the family; as a nurse, a secretary or a teacher.

Matron and nurse at a hospital in Juba, Southern Sudan.

Secretary to a managing director, Ghana.

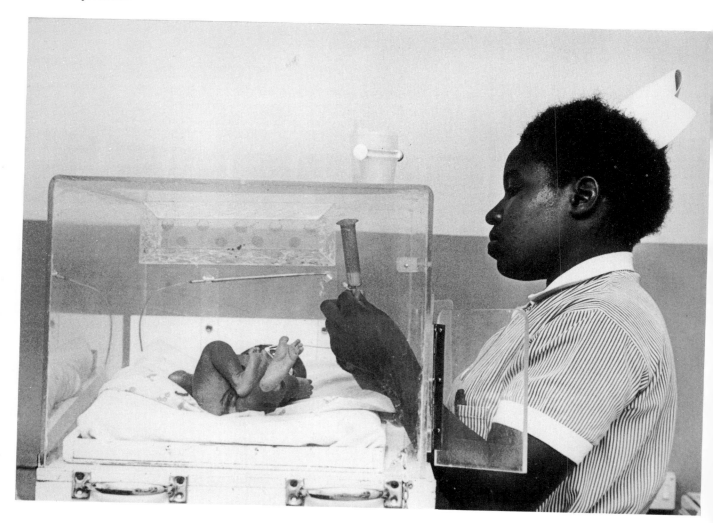

Nursing a premature baby in
a locally constructed incubator,
Mvumi, Tanzania.

Secretary in a shipping firm,
Dar-es-Salaam, Tanzania.

Teaching music at Ringway
Estate School for Girls, Accra,
Ghana. Relatively few of these
girls will go to secondary school.

Teaching basic literacy to teenage girls. Sabtinga, Upper Volta.

Joyce Foli, Secretary of a Consumer Co-op, at a local market in Ghana. She has been on several educational and training programmes in Russia. More women are beginning to join the many African men who go each year for training in China, Russia, Cuba and Israel.

Politics and influence

'Women have some power at local level — but not beyond that.'
●Buchi Emecheta

'Certain older women in villages become very independent and respected. Christianity shook this attitude very badly. It was not considered nice or feminine to speak out. But the dignity which African women had and which was lost during colonisation is coming back.'
● Buchi Emecheta

Irim village, Upper Volta. Welcome ceremony and discussion with development workers on possible projects for the village. Arguments were made for a medical programme, literacy teaching and agricultural support.

Women's meeting Boundoum
Nord, Senegal.

Street election rally. Nairobi, Kenya. Kenya has a one-party system so these women will vote to select an official Kenyan African National Union (KANU) candidate.

75

The council of Kwa Mkono Ujamaa village, Tanzania. In 1967 President Julius Nyere committed his country to a policy of development through rural socialism. In the vanguard were to be the *ujamaa* villages based on the traditional African extended family and the idea of collective work. Despite problems with the programme it has influenced socialist thinking throughout Africa and the rest of the world.

'The men sit on chairs — the women and children on the floor. It is symbolic. Even in Tanzania and at local level.'
● *Buchi Emecheta*

Family structures

'In much of the world, marriage, which is considered a sign of adulthood and is viewed as an institution to be respected, is consequently an event to be looked forward to and celebrated ... Yet for many women it is a point at which control over a woman's life passes from her father to her husband.'
● Helvi Sipila

'. . . the new care of children in the cities is different from that in the village. The children have no compounds to belong to. They all cramp into one room with mother alone acting as the mother, the father, the compound head, the grandmother and all those community relatives of the extended family which a village child has as its birthright.'
● *Buchi Emecheta*

Agnes Kidera is a tenant squatter in Mathare Valley, the shanty town district of Nairobi. She moved from the country to join her husband in the search for work. She now brings up her 11 children alone. More than one third of her wages goes on rent for one room 10ft x 12ft. It has no water, sanitation, lighting or heating. The rest of her income is spent on essentials such as water, food, clothing and the school fees for five children.

'In agrarian societies polygamous life works because there are more hands to work on the farm. Also no child is without a family like the cases one reads in developed countries.'
● *Buchi Emecheta*

'... in some cases where there are more than three wives the senior wife is not expected to take part in cooking at all. The senior wife is thus in a privileged position. The fact that she is free from tedious farming work and the boring carrying and fetching of water and cooking for a large family leaves her time to concentrate on developing her personality. If she is lucky to be blessed with sons she becomes a very strong person in her family and is respected in the community.'
● *Buchi Emecheta*

'You can inherit your brother's wife and even your father's wife if she is still young – that is, can still bear children.'
● *Buchi Emecheta*

'... In traditional society, economic possessions are almost absent. It was more important to satisfy biological, social and religious needs.

'One acquires goods to ward off shame'
... Education aims at developing self-control, resistance to difficulty.

Friendship is a positive value. *'If you enter a friend's hut, you will sleep better than in the hut of relatives'.*

Solidarity is cultivated by practice and by proverbs. *'Those who leave on the same day will not overtake each other'.*

Report on Co-operatives in Upper Volta. Bernard Ouedraogo

'This is how it ought to be. But he'll say that when he's free he'll free her.
● *Buchi Emecheta*

Traditional societies

'The older a woman gets the more respect she commands . . . Her words are listened to with reverence and her daughters-in-law leave their children with her . . .

'Most of these village functions are now being eroded. Old ladies in the urban city centres are becoming headaches for their offspring due to scarcity of adequate accommodation.'
● *Buchi Emecheta*

There have been many highly sophisticated and strong nations in Africa throughout its history. The great empires of Benin and Ashanti are examples of two which flourished in West Africa. The Masai, like the Zulus are warriors. They live in what are now Kenya and Tanzania. They consider farming beneath them but they keep large herds of cattle. Both women and men are proud and independent. Young women select lovers from amongst the *moran* (young warriors). The jewellery she wears often indicates a woman's status. When she marries she wears long beaded rings in pierced ears; when her son becomes a warrior she wears the flat spiral decorations shown in the photograph. Men and boys care for the cattle. Women run the household, raise children and build huts.

A Tanzanian potter. In many parts of Africa women make the pots essential for cooking, storage and carrying water. It is a highly-regarded craft.

'Ethiopia. Telling stories to children and smoking one or two pipes; lap stretched, sitting well, legs held together. Beautifying the body is well emphasized in most traditional African societies. Jewellery may look heavy to the western observer, but most of our 'jewels' were made from parts of animals until the love for precious stones took over.'
● *Buchi Emecheta*

'. . . in her traditional society she had a role, a difficult one, but still a role that made her feel like a person in her community . . . now . . . such roles are being denied her . . . now she is caught in the middle between the traditional and the modern.'
● *Buchi Emecheta*

Education and training

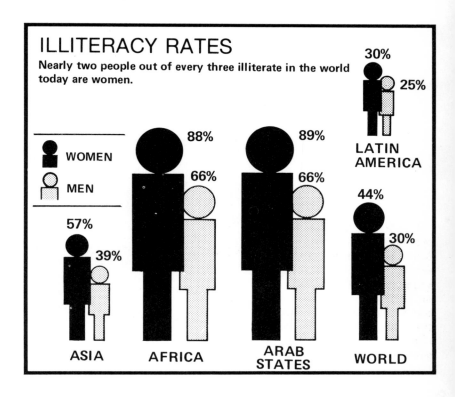

ILLITERACY RATES

Nearly two people out of every three illiterate in the world today are women.

WOMEN

MEN

30%
25%
LATIN AMERICA

88%
66%

89%
66%

57%
39%

44%
30%

ASIA

AFRICA

ARAB STATES

WORLD

From birth girls are conditioned into second-class citizenship; in Africa, in Europe, in the rest of the world. They are programmed into fulfilling subordinate and supporting roles – to men. They get fewer educational opportunities and at school are subtly channelled into 'soft' subjects and away from subjects like maths, physics, chemistry and engineering. The process is reinforced from many directions: through the media; because women teachers are seen to have less status than men teachers; and because less is expected intellectually of girls at school. So many women never fulfil their potential, and particular female gifts are not used to enrich those jobs and professions which are still male closed shops.

'*She could do with a watering can. Even though both boys and girls do farming practice she will be the one who stays in the village and does farm work. The boys are more mobile and leave.*'
● *Buchi Emecheta*

In Tanzanian schools agricultural practice is part of the curriculum. At this school the pupils grow maize, bananas, vegetables, cassava, beans and cotton. Most of the food is used in school lunches which are free. Any surplus is sold and the money put in the school fund.

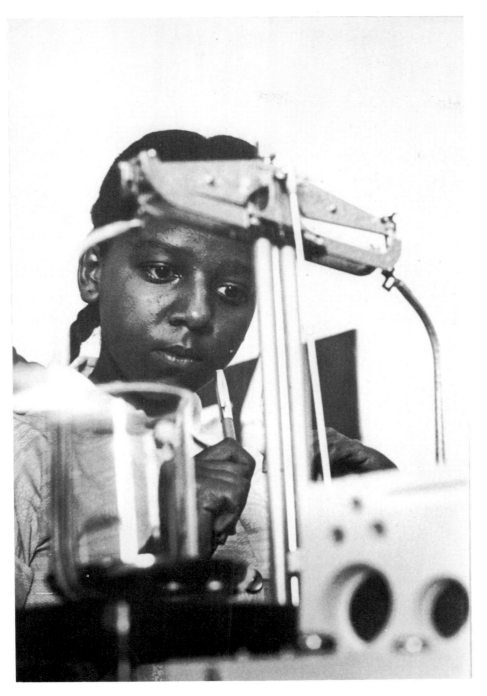

'For every girl here at school there are two or three at home helping the mother.'
● *Buchi Emecheta*

Science class. Ethiopia.

In Africa many countries are committed to universal education but economic difficulties often make it hard to maintain that commitment. Kenya and Tanzania both spend over one quarter of their national budgets, in different ways, on education. Nevertheless, many children do not get a place in school until they are twelve or thirteen. Girls tend to lose out more than boys in these circumstances.

Doing homework. Egypt.

'Many West African countries are now introducing free primary education. It is not compulsory in all African countries and parents are free to make a choice. Would a girl be more useful helping her mother at home or in her market trade or would she benefit from education... could the family afford the fees? And how long should she stay at school.'
● *Buchi Emecheta*

Teacher training examination. Ethiopia.

Adult literacy class. Eastleigh Centre in a poor district of Nairobi.

Development and aid

'. . . economic development is often still talked about as if it was mainly a subject for men. Plans and projects are designed by men to be implemented by men on the assumption that if men, as the heads of households, benefit from these projects, the women and the children in those households will benefit too. Women's problems still tend to be regarded as separate, rather than as facets of the culture and structure of all societies . . . UN statistics also underestimate the number of households in which the woman is the *de facto* economic head because they use biassed definitions of head-of-the-household instead of a criterion reflecting actual economic contributions. Thus women remain statistically invisible. Yet their contributions are indispensable and basic.'

● Brandt report.

'... men hold overwhelming control over the proceeds of labour both in the rural and urban settings. How does this happen? First, traditional patriarchal values still have a very real hold over the society. Secondly, due to colonial and post-independence government policies, as well as the biases of employers, men hold a monopoly over job opportunities.'
● Mariam Matiko in *New African*.

101

The Women's Group of Ofrey Village, Yatenga, Upper Volta building a storehouse for communal grain stocks. Their group is based on the traditional associations for communal work called *Nam*.

'Nam in the territory of the Mossi people, is a traditional organisation with multiple functions: economic, political (in the sense of teaching the laws which govern the society), cultural and social.'
● World Council of Churches Sahel Team booklet.

Some of the *Nam* groups in Yatenga have been helped with their projects by government and international agencies. As a development model the *Nam* experiment is highly successful, probably because the projects have always been controlled by the villagers themselves and the organization is rooted in existing village structures. Projects include constructing wells, clinics and mills; running market gardens, growing crops and breeding animals; and even village theatricals.

Member of Ofrey Village Women's Group. See previous page.

Solar cookers were intro-
duced into Zimtanga Village,
Upper Volta, by UNDPC and
Danchurch Aid. They were
designed in Denmark and the
reflecting bowls manufactured
there. The women of the village
did not ask for them. Although
they save fuel-gathering time,
they are not used much because
they have many shortcomings.
These, which became obvious
soon after installation, are as
follows:
* They are large and wobbly
  and so clutter up the
  courtyard.
* Most cooking in Africa is
  done after sunset.
* The structure needs re-
  setting every ¼ hour to
  follow the sun.
* They only take a small
  cooking pot – unsuitable for
  family meals.
* They will only function with
  a metal pot, not the earthen-
  ware pots owned by most
  people.
* It is difficult to cook *tog*
  sauce (a common food in
  Upper Volta) on such a flimsy
  structure because this
  requires energetic stirring.

The cookers will, in fact, be
modified, but it would have
been simpler if the women
who were going to use them
had been consulted in the first
place. Alternatively, they could
have been designed locally in
nearby Bamako or Abidjan
where there are solar research
stations.

Mayers' Ranch, 30 miles from Nairobi, Kenya. Tourists come by mini-bus at 3 o'clock every day to see the famous garden round the farmhouse. After tea they can photograph the Masai women and warriors who are permitted to live on the ranch in return for daily 'performances' of their dancing and way of life.

For some countries tourism seems a simple means of earning foreign exchange. It has some advantages but it can also lead to social, economic and environmental disadvantages.

It is difficult to write about birth control and sexuality in cultures other than our own. The most we can hope to do is understand that complex economic, historic and emotional factors are involved. In some cultures large families are an economic necessity and not, as often claimed, the result of fecklessness or ignorance. Children work from a very early age and act as an economic insurance policy for the future. So where there is a high death rate amongst children families have to be larger. But this is not, as some commentators see it, the end of the story. Some women in Africa would like to have *smaller* families, but their husbands are against it. It may be financial arguments and traditional attitudes to fatherhood and virility which influence the men. It is the real burdens of birth and childcare which affect the women. In Africa as in Europe women still take the main responsibility for childrearing and they are beginning to voice the feeling that because of this they should have control over their own bodies and a greater influence over the size of their family.

107

For over two hundred years we have been told what the 'true' situation is in numerous books about Africa. The openly racist attitudes of the day aside there are clear references to the amount of work that women do. In many books it is commented on in passing but then, as now, the economic importance and other implications attaching to it are ignored.

'. . . the men of the village go out to the village farm, cut away the jungle with their butcher's knives and leave the brush to dry in the hot sun. Then it is set on fire and man's work is o'er. The planting, the care of the growing crop, the gathering and the milling is woman's work' *The Land of the White Helmet*, Forbes 1910

Women are responsible for over half the agricultural production in Africa.

Afterword

On a photographic trip to West Africa I travelled with one of the few women field staff working for a development agency. Years previously, in a village which was part of a United Nations Women's Project she had asked the women what they thought of the project. Their response was clear. 'Oh them,' they said, 'They come to the village, talk to the men and then go away again. They never speak to us.' From that point she determined never to visit a village again without talking to women.

Working with her, taking pictures and listening to women express their point of view was an education for me. This book started then. In villages all over Africa I have sat in circles and listened to women's lives being interpreted by men. Sometimes by foreign development agents, sometimes by local aid workers and sometimes by village men themselves. In Upper Volta though, the women did the talking. They spoke about health, about literacy, about farming and everything else that concerned their lives. They spoke from their own everyday experiences. Gradually, I began to realize that I had been as guilty as anyone else in the way I had photographed and selected images of African women for more than thirteen years. I had the Western attitude which devalues women's work and ignores their central contribution to their own economies. I had accepted men's interpretations of African women's work and lives.

Photography has been used to exploit or misrepresent many peoples outside the modern, industrialised economies of the West. The African view is that most photographs are taken of them to ridicule and oversimplify their culture. They know photographers earn large sums of money by presenting them as exotic fodder for colour magazines or as emaciated victims with no autonomy or skills.

This book aims to present a different view. Buchi Emecheta's Nigerian experience sets the pictures in an African context. Her observations have shaped the selection and illuminated meanings and details within the pictures. The relationship between the images and the text are crucial; they are not separate.

Because photography can be voyeuristic I prefer to work where people know what I am doing and why. Ideally, I have been able to stay in a village for some days, talking to groups of people about the photographs I want to take before actually taking any. In most situations it is essential to be accompanied by a guide or interpreter. It is quite possible to take 'candid' photographs on the streets of almost any city or big town in the world, but if you want to get off the streets or into a rural community you cannot just walk in anywhere with two Nikons slung round your neck and a pocketful of film.

Photography's role as a tool of communication can easily be over-rated. It is very good at documenting tangible things but it cannot illustrate abstract ideas on its own. It can show clearly the kind of house someone lives in but not the social and economic reasons for them living in it. It can show what a Tanzanian *ujamaa* village looks like but not the socialist ideals which formed it and support it. It is necessary to look at pictures in relation to caption, text or information from other sources.

Photography is essentially a process of selection. First of all the photographer selects a subject, then decides how to record it; what angle to shoot from, whether to use colour or black and white, wide angle lens or telephoto. All these things affect the 'reading' of a picture a final audience will make.

There are many subjects which are rarely, if ever, selected for photography. In Kenya, for example, I could have chosen to record big game, or to photograph the Masai as warriors rather than the tourist attractions that some of them are becoming. Such choices are usually characterised as 'personal', 'individual' or 'creative'. In fact, they are culturally formed and stem from a bias or framework which the photographer brings to every exposure. Thus there is no way in which photographs can be considered to be objective.

When I look through the photographs I have taken in Africa over a number of years I can very clearly see bias at work. As my own socialism and feminism have developed the subjects of the photographs and the way they are presented has changed. More and more women appear and they are no longer just standing picturesquely with children on their hips but working, hoeing, weeding and watering. I had become aware that African women were not always mothers and wives alone, but farmers, traders and providers.

In her book *The Domestication of Women*, Barbara Rogers has documented how discrimination affects poor women in the non-Western world. In an article for the United Nations during International Women's Year she wrote, 'The policies of international agencies and "development" institutions have remained, in the face of all the evidence, based on the assumption that only men are of economic importance; and that they as "heads of households", are the proper recipients of all development benefits such as cash, employment, training, credit, extension services and the rest'.

The courage of the women of Eretrea, Azania (South Africa) and Zimbabwe has been well recorded. Even the world's press has had to recognise their dedication in taking up arms to defend their homes, their children, their way of life and their political ideals. They are not isolated, unique examples of the strength of African women. The particular circumstances of their oppression have forced them to take extremely radical positions. But in their day to day lives the majority of African women show equal determination, self-reliance and economic independence. What they lack are political power and recognition of their rights.

Maggie Murray, March 1981

Book List of further reading

The Domestication of Women, Barbara Rogers, 1980, Kogan Page.
The Slave Girl, Buchi Emecheta, 1977, Fontana Paperback.
The Bride Price, Buchi Emecheta, 1976, Fontana Paperback.
The Joys of Motherhood, Buchi Emecheta, 1979, Heinemann African Writers Series.
Idu, Flora Nwapa, 1970, Heinemann African Writers Series.
Women under Apartheid, Photographs and text. 1981, International Defence and Aid Fund.
Choices in Development – Kenya and Tanzania, 1975
Living with the Land – Ghana, 1977
Education photo-packs. Ikon Productions, Distributed by CWDE 128 Buckingham Palace Road, London SW1.

New Internationalist, Monthly magazine about development issues.
New African, Monthly magazine.
Spare Rib, Monthly women's liberation magazine with occasional articles about women in Africa.
International Development Studies Bulletin, Monthly from the University of Sussex. Articles about current research and debate on development themes.